Bonne Annee
Of Success, Life, and Poetry

Yasmin S Brown

Bonne Année

Of Success, Life, and Poetry

© Yasmin S. Brown

ISBN 978-1-962374-45-3 Paperback

ISBN 978-1-962374-46-0 eBook

Library of Congress Control Number: 2025907460

Published by Prolific Pulse Press LLC

Contact: admin@prolificpulse.com

Raleigh, North Carolina USA

May 2025

DEDICATION

This book is dedicated to everyone striving to make it one more year around the sun.

Table of Contents

ACKNOWLEDGMENTS

I thank Zan Johns for writing the Foreword and being my poetry mentor.

I appreciate the support of my children and niece for providing reviews and feedback.

Thank you to my publisher and editor for bringing my words to life for the readers.

FOREWORD

Zaneta Varnado Johns

Bonne Annee is a stirring invitation to embrace life fully and at every opportunity, to start anew. Poet Yasmin S Brown has a unique style—free verse and rhythm iced with the presence of her literary traditions. She is unapologetic and creative. Each expression leaves you eager for the next. Prepare for expressive wit and surprise.

Brown's devoutness is tightly and brightly woven throughout. From the title, Bonne Annee, you will anticipate the start of a new year no matter the season. Poems provide hope and inspiration, a poetic therapy of sorts. Restoration beckons. Nature calls. Dreams blossom. Authentic expressions about love are featured in "Eclipsed Love" and "Unspoken Love." Messages about life are beautifully contrasted with nature's forces of rain, fog, wind, fire, and sand. I particularly salute "Wind," a lyrical force to be reckoned with.

Brown reveals her deepest connection to God in "In Hide and Seek," where her spiritual clarity is indisputable. Her commendable work with women's empowerment is delivered through Power Her Forward LLC. Without knowledge of this organization, I declared her shortest expression "R.O.A.R." to be one of the longest messages of transformation and peace. In four concise lines, Brown captures her life's mission as described in her words, "She utilizes literacy to encourage women to move forward through the concept of R.O.A.R. (Restoration, Overcome, Awareness, Resilience)."

Gravitational Pull of Nature

Night Moon

Sitting under the midnight moon,
Reflecting on a day gone too soon,
As I grow weary of your aspirations,
Winding down with a glass of wine.

Observing my dream through imagination and
observation,
With freedom of liberation,
And illumination circling the atmosphere,
With the guidance of a silent night,

Whispering under the brightness of universal
prognostication,
Relaxing with the glowing light of your
circumference,
The darkness is no longer scary, but oh-so-bright,
Full of good intentions.

Finding clarity,
Among the daily noise of life,
Through the quietness of an occasional whistling of
the wind,
A howling wolf can be heard in the dark,
Tonight's full moon sets the stage even though we
are miles apart.

Park

Sitting in the park,
Listening and watching my surroundings,
As birds chirp perched on tree branches while the
squirrels rustle bright green leaves,
To the sound of crickets behind those trees.

Sitting in the park,
Hearing yells and screams,
Of softball cheers and children rounding the bases,
"Tink!" goes the metal bat across the round white
ball,
"Run, run!" the coach call.

Sitting in the park,
With the sound of creaking swing chains,
Youth loudly giggling,
As they throw sand from the sandbox.

Sitting in the park,
While dogs walk by,
Barking with their master,
Alert for protection staring in my direction.

Sitting in the park,
At a garden party,
Enjoying the gentle breeze,
While glancing at the sunset from the horizon,
Leaving the park,
As it is now becoming dark.

Balcony View

Sitting on the balcony,
Meditating facing the rays of the sun,
As it shares its vitamin D,
Rebooting my energy.

With the undertone of birds tweeting,
And the speed of flapping wings,
Nature draws my attention,
To gently float among Cottonwood seeds.

Parasailing to the buzzing of bees,
Followed by the various cars zooming by,
With each unique sound,
Under the grunting of a frog tone.

I listen, as I sip my coffee,
To the bouncing of a basketball,
As the children slowly walk past,
In sync with every step of a cricket's wings,

Orchestrated by the branches of trees,
Swaying of the grass,
Each morning, I witness,
The memories from the balcony were imprinted in
my view.

Clouds

Lying in my backyard on blades of greenery,
Gazing off into the great beyond of my scenery,
Losing focus as time rolls by,
Finding myself lost in a place among the clouds,
A series of dreams of fluffy white pillows,
Gliding ever so softly,
Creating a motion of inspirational sprout,
Planting seeds with long nurturing roots.

Feeding my new beginnings,
From a beautiful backdrop of clear blue skies,
With birds flapping by,
Placing a photograph in my imagination of harvested
fruits.

Endless destinations,
Illustrated by the dangling motivation of tropical
land, blue water, and tan sand,
Lucid dreams of a matrix,
Opening and closing doors,
leaving visible scars like a cicatrix.

Lessons of Nature

Listening to the wind as it blows
Observing those who pass by,
As the wind grows quiet,
And the waterfalls,

Into a leaking faucet,
Of birds chirping,
soggy leaves and insects flying away with the
breeze,
I am drowning in the quietness,

Along with the beauty of the universal dwelling,
Nature's bliss with a creative twist,
A trail to the imagination,
With every sway of a tree,

Rooted with the universe teaching thee,
stop, sit, and listen to me,
the wisdom of a plant's roots,
Embedded in a calm stream.

Of flowing nutrition,
Like a harmonious collection of multicolored fronds,
In a stationary position,
With every gust from beyond,

The unknown variable is what you believe.

Nature's Waltz

In the darkness of the night,
Stood barren tall trees,
Full of hope,
That one day, their leaves will regrow.

With the richness of the soil,
And solid foundation,
Standing in the rain,
Absorbing streamlined water flowing from the gutter
drain.

Accompanied by the delight of the daylight sun,
Shining through the leaflets,
Of the swaying branches,
dancing as though they were ballroom dancers.

Waltzing after every drink,
In performance with Mother Nature,
Smooth as a nectarine,
A fruit of an expression of elegance,

With the rise and fall of the sun.

Quietness Of a Prairie

"Shh, be quiet!"
Enjoy my beauty in silence,
Observing in contemplation,
Taking every space in.

The endless blades of grass,
Watching butterflies pass by,
Popping of the dandelions,
Under the horizon sun.

Shh, be quiet!
I just saw a prairie dog ...it was a little one,
Nibbling on the sea of greens and yellows,
Aww, I whispered a soft hello,

Quietness of prairie,
A place of grounding with the universe,
Frolicking in the grass,
Leaving my shoes on the path.

Shh, be quiet!
Stressed and I can no longer hide it,
Quietness of a prairie,
This is where my stress subsides.

Resilience of a Bird

The resilience of a bird,
Is durable yet swift,
Gliding through the sky,
Once Mama said it was time to fly.

Overcoming the obstacle,
With sounds of a soft flutter,
Flapping melodies of freedom,
Providing hope of something better,

Centered from above,
Grounded ever so sturdy,
Sitting calm perch among the greenery,
Peaceful as pure as a dove.

Tapping into its capacity,
healing from a broken wing,
Fight or flight after adversity,
Learning to fly again,

Flexible with flexibility,
Feeling the caress of the breeze,
Rediscovering the voice of agility,
Sustaining with elasticity,

Chirping with the resilience of a bird remarkable and recovering.

Solar Legacy

Through time and space,
My life cannot be erased,
Like the chalk on a chalkboard,
The particles fly into outer space.

Floating, touching things all round,
Clapping together with a loud echo sound,
An atom creating everything around me,
Building an unbreakable legacy.

 A solar system within the galaxy,
One plus two equals three,
Scientific equation,
Made with a variety.

Bell curving possibilities,
A calculus of means and medians,
Studying through every experience,
Light years expressed through Planeteers,

Time and space you have been the legacy that is
never misplaced.

Universal Soul Connection

Although I cannot see you,
I am embraced in your radiant aura,
Glowing like the funnel of illumination through
darkness,
My guiding light you make everything all right.

Connecting me to the universe,
Putting my mental health first,
Sharing your tranquility of calmness,
Alluring beauty is full of power.

Harmonizing in harmony,
Keeping me grounded under my feet,
At any time or place, I am in your colorful space,
Feeling each blade of grass, my heart rate slows
down fast,

With the luminosity of the NorthStar,
Directing you with the righteousness to go far,
You are my universal connection,
Protecting me with grace and protection.

Waterfall

Oh! waterfall you relax me,
Bringing self-care,
With your constancy,
Of a calm demeanor,

When no one else is there,
You inspire my creativity,
Pulling out the best things,
Expressions of good intentions,

Oh! waterfall with your beckoned call,
Stopping everyone to listen,
To your calm or roaring disposition,
With your hyaline essence.

The provenance of a flow inside and out,
Providing nutrition for every living thing,
Rehydration to dehydration, cleanse to disdain,
making everything clean,
within your Divine purpose.

New Roots

The first time I laid eyes on you,
Your existence overwhelmed my view,
Acquiring the joy inside of me,
Breathing a new root like a freshly planted tree,

Branching out on a journey of discovery,
Embracing change as though you were an Autumn
leaf,
Painting beauty like an art gallery expedition,
Taking my breath with the stroke of your scenery.

Fresh start with diverse precision,
A quest with no need for introduction,
Bringing colorful opportunities,
Overcoming stains of browning greens,

Closing the chapter on two thousand twenty-three,
Making necessary adjustments,
As you open the door to two thousand twenty-four,
Shedding every leaf that holds you back from being
repurposed and free.

Intersection of Life

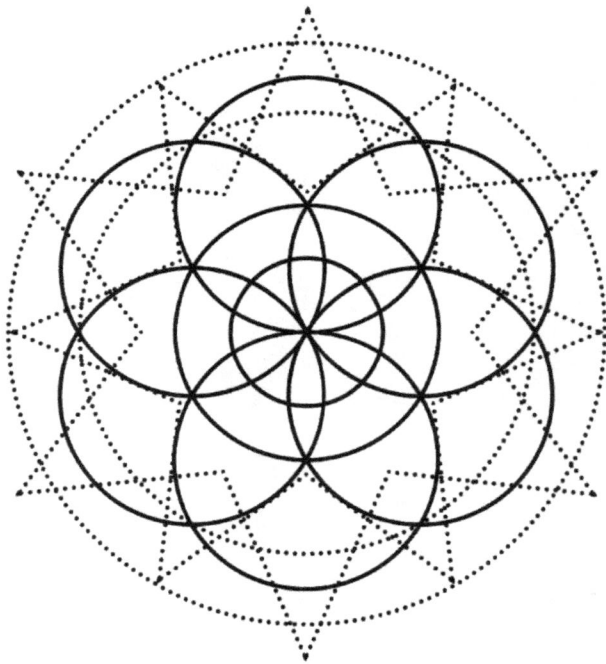

The Table

What do you bring to the table?
You pull up the table,
I will bring you the chairs,
Showing you how much I care.

You bring the groceries,
I will prepare the meal,
Serving a king with so many dreams.

The world gives you stress,
I provide you with peace,
Massaging you fast asleep,

You bring a business idea,
I help create a plan,
Supporting the execution of your vision helping you be
in demand,

You bring a problem,
I help you find a solution,
Bouncing ideas until you choose one.

Mind

My mind flows like a body of water,
Smooth and clean as if it were a suit from the cleaners,
Pimping downstream with thoughts and ideas,
Envisioning through visualization a unique vision of
execution,

Regardless of how fast or slow your thoughts passing
out ads like newspapers,
Circulating currents of a river around a log obstruction,
Locking together the past and present.

As though it was the end in mind,
Minding the end of a legacy,
that did not begin or end with me,
A generational ancestry is ongoing if we could be,
Building futures like beavers to dams,

Sticking to the plan,
Like gum under a desk,
Scrapping the surface and understanding you are worth
it.

Compassion of a Shoe

Shoes are meant to be filled,
Walked on and displayed,
Taken care of even when gently worn,
Literally or figuratively,
Despite its journey.

Walking in someone else's shoes,
Considering all the things they have been through,
Supporting you as a stand-up person,
Full of concern with your purpose.

Showing mercy through goodwill,
Often discarded because of wear and tear,
Understanding not just where you have been,
but also, where you're going,
There and then,
I share my compassion with you as more than one shoe
just for you Good-natured with benevolence.

To Do

Small steps,
Big dreams,
Benchmarks to accomplish.

Set goals,
Complete tasks,
A sagacious future has yet to unfold,

Big picture,
20/20 vision,
Discovering that the purpose of life is to serve.

Mission accomplished,
Projects complete,
A successful and pyrrhic satisfaction.

Zesty

Getting zesty,
With my bestie,
Bringing out the bubbly,
Starting a new year is not messy.

Sailing through life, doing what is best for me,
Preserving and protecting my energy,
Prognosticating my journey,
Taking chances to renew my vitality.

Releasing balloons of adversity,
While building universal ascendancy,
Connecting like a special delivery,
Sign, sealed in victory.

Darkness

In the darkness, I wait,
As my conscience shared
Everything I have grown to fear,
From the rushing of thoughts in deafening silence.

In the darkness, I wait,
Overwhelmed without thinking clearly,
With incomplete feelings attempting to overpower me,
Sharing past traumatic memories.

In the darkness, I fought,
What was causing stress to my body,
Subconsciously conversing what was suppressing who I
could be,
Working to devour and leave me shoddy.

In the darkness,
Ducking a fist,
Followed by a flick of the wrist,
Right hook, left hook leaving me shaken in the mist,

Out of the darkness,
I cannot let it go from bad to worse,
As the spiral wants to take me out in the hearse,
Suppressing the negative sounds.

In the darkness,
Standing strong, triumphant in victory,
With the help of God's positive energy,
Prevailing with perseverance,
It was shining through darkness willingly.

Roll-O-Coaster

Flutter, flutter goes the butterflies in my stomach,
As I stand in line observing the amusement park,
With nostrils full of fresh cotton candy, buttery popcorn,
and Sandy's caramel candies,
My eyes gloss over to the smiles of joy of every little boy
and girl,

Waiting for boarding, we are up next,
Taking a seat to click the seat belts,
Tightly embracing the safety bars,
Secured in each little car.

In preparation for the ascent,
The sound of the lift chain means we are all in,
To climax to the first drop,
Released in the g-force,

Going sixty seconds non-stop,
Longitude and latitude to bend and turn,
As my body bangs and squirms,
Full of excitement as the ride comes to an end,

Roll-o-coaster I want to get on again!

Archery

There is no one like you,
To draw on my energy,
Committed to discipline,
Trained in alignment,

On one accord through resistance and strength,
Pulling back from dysfunction,
Steadily consistent in conjunction,
With the aim of an arrow, purpose for length.

Going the distance,
Charging like a bull,
Purpose-filled on fire,
Running as though you saw red in a bull's eye,

Targeting with depth and perception,
Beginning like a beginner,
Advance in the advancement,
 You are the future winner,

As you successfully balance your arch,
Show appreciation for the past and present,
Gifting the atmosphere with your presence,
Keeping your composure with accuracy and precision.

Listen

There is a numinous power,
Setting in silence for hours,
Opening your mind to the door of honesty,
With yourself when there is no one else,

To control the co-sign of what you made up in your
mind,
Because the truth is always right on time,
Clocking the will and way to get things done,
In a way, which is conducive to benefit you.

Like nourishment to your body let it come through,
To bring out the chutzpah in you,
Unwavering with patience,
Believing in what you do,

Listening to your thoughts inside of you,
With a focus on your inner conversation,
Dictating a new narration,
Aligning mind, body, and soul,
Without judgment until you reach the end of your goal.

Fear

Do not fear me because I do not look like you, walk like
you, talk,
like you, or act like you.
Do not allow the ignorance of someone,
Create a barrier like me to cause you to fear me.

 For I am an intellectual,
intelligent, smart with a lot of heart.
Will rise to the occasion without
hesitation.
Others' perception of me will not create fear and
despair in the air.

I am a loving soul with an inventive mind
 Know more about me to remove your fear
 Let us get into the grove
Move this country to a better place...
Not just the thought,
of one race—that is a disgrace.

We are here not to compare,
But to share love and peace.
Work toward unity
Then violence will cease.

Road

As I sit at the back of the bus watching the road through
the front
windshield,
I notice the road is a lot like life's journey with faith
Sometimes you have a straight shot through your
voyage.
Then at other times, there are curves or stops in the
road.

Every road guides you to your destination
No matter how many stops and turns you make.

God lets us know He will guide our every step
Through the rain, fog, sun, wind, fire, and even fear,
If only we just believe with
the faith of mustard seed.

A Conversation with My Soul

Why is my energy disrupted?
You see your energy is like a battery,
Running on electricity,
Causing static between you and me,

Sparking your aura and tranquility,
Changing your positivity,
Energizing everyone you meet,
Disrupting your possibilities.

Of growth and development,
the dreams that you have are heaven-sent,
Crossing paths with your soul,
Channeling energy like a beta blocker,

Building a chemical imbalance what a shocker,
Making our connection grow silent,
Producing bridges of chaos,
Having your mind and body at odds,

Safeguard your vitality with protection,
Reconstructing the negative destruction,
Climbing ladders of inferiority,
Breaking barriers gives hope to those who believe.

Acknowledge there is separation,
Overcome with mental health preparation,
Align mind, body, and soul,
In that order, your spirit will intensify,
A conversation with my soul was powerful and
inspirational.

Discipline

Where, oh where did my discipline go,
Did it melt away with winter snow?
As a result of breaking my New Year's resolution,
resulting in not keeping up with the tradition.

Even though preparations were done with good
intentions,
Realizing tangible progress was missing,
Good health and fortune,
Whoops! Did I forget to mention?

The two pounds I wanted to lose,
Stuck around every time I hit snooze,
Oh, where, oh, where did my discipline go?
Nonetheless starting over with possibilities to grow,

Pruning leaves as if I were a weeping willow,
A tree full of dramatics,
Elegant with my status,
Utilizing my healing properties to rebuild the discipline,
Bravo!

Emotions

When my emotions get the best of me,
I want to be set free,
Like wings on a plane,
gliding in the rain,
With a realization I can fly,

Set a goal,
Plan,
Execute what others may not understand,
Visualize your dream
You are what the world has been missing.

Being emotionally set free,
Healing through creativity,
Painting your feelings,
Expressing what is unappealing.

A dictation of peace,
Setting your soul to release,
Pain and sorrow,
Allowing space and acceptance for tomorrow.

Life is a process,
Compassion and work in progress,
Adaptability and altitude,
Setting boundaries for negative attitudes

Your emotions are set free!

A Negativity Burial

Here lies my thoughts,
Lying flat on the ground,
In a million pieces,
Staring up at me without uttering a sound.

Pain, hurt, and defeat,
Bounce back, bounce back!
You are not weak,
You are a warrior with so much depth.

Ten toes deep,
Until there is nothing left,
In dry soiled dirt,
Laying to rest.

Words of my past,
With a plaque that reads,
"The darkness failed; positive energy succeeded."

Burying the rain from the prior forecast,
Predicting a new narrative,
Letting go of things that will not last,
Mapping a Future Elaborative.

Rebuilding with a Divine purpose,
Striving to reclaim more than just,
the surface,
My soul and spirit,
A heart full of love, can you hear it?

Understanding my worth,
You have had value since birth,
currency man cannot give,
Outstanding merit to live,

A burial of negative words, and thoughts

You are free as a jailbird!

Life Cycle

In the beginning, there dawns something new,
Unknown of what is true,
A thought, creation withstanding duration,
Of what could be what should be.

The circle of life is a mirror and dream,
A futuristic reflection,
Floating of your salvation,
Delivering you a vision.

Astigmatism of correction,
Blindsided by the noise of transgression,
Silencing the test of your testimonies,
Vocalizing one's desires at ceremonies.

A place of restoration
Putting pieces back together in incomplete spaces,
Rebuilding yourself brick by brick until your destination,
Wearing down to submission and retreat.

Restarting with the end in mind,
Developing habits like Dr. Stephen R Covey's,
Changing the perception of one's grind,
A task, project, and purpose of an individual's recovery,

Teaching people what was learned throughout life's
journey.

Life's Flood

When lightning lights up the sky,
And the rumble of thunder rolls by,
The pain of the universe starts to fall.

Drops of tears from the clouds
Bustle through the streets with a stride,
Showing a force like a raging rapid ride,
Knocking objects off course.

Showing bad intentions without remorse,
Destroying foundations leaving nothing but memories,
Sounds of yelling when there is no choice,
Leaving adroit people to clean up the aftermath.

Flooding life with adversity that can never be solved
easily.

Reflection

A sheet of glass smudged in environmental imprints,
Cracked at the center of what you see,
Sharing reflections that look like me.

Full of pain, strain, unhinged and drained,
Shattered pieces,
Swept up and thrown away,
Superglued for another day,

Alone, searching my soul,
On a quest to find a better me, the only "me,"
To fill the people around me.

I am at mental capacity,
Bandaging the beginner,
Gauzing the center,
As rock bottom is the winner.

An inference of change,
Heating and rebuilding,
Utilizing a piece of inner diversity,
Past, Present, and Future me.

Creating a masterpiece unfiltered,
Shoved in a burning inferno,
Rebirthing a phenomenal phoenix,
Emerging with alterations.

Burning in self-awareness,
Glowing with emotional intelligence,
Breaking glass is like a traumatic experience,

My reflection is not what you see,
But resilience is inside of me.

Love

Eclipsed Love

As my heartbeat rises,
In your celestial presents,
With the shadow of your silhouette,
Owning the perception of my ocular view.

Obscuring my thoughts,
Like an eclipse of the sun,
If only for a minute,
To illustrate the chicanery of futuristic plans.

Blinding the eyes of those,
Who cannot imagine you and me in the future,
Sharing a love so strong, in sync like the hands on a
clock,
No matter how much time passed, we still held on.

For twenty-four hours my imagination was with you,
To meet someday soon,
Underneath the eclipse of the moon,
Until I open my eyes to see you are no longer in the
room.

Structure of Love

Love is a verb and noun,
It is felt all around,
Regardless of gender or race,
It is shared through time and space.

Intending to act,
Causing a chain reaction,
Of intensity full of emotions,
Distributing sacrifice and devotion.

A meaningful transaction,
It forgives like the separation of water,
Goes deep as a scuba diver in a wetsuit,
And express it as though it was graffiti on a structural
partition.

A wall built with sadness and defeat,
Broken down by unconditional love on repeat,
Bouncing back like children on a trampoline,
Jumping through the rings of healing with the purpose of
a well-oiled machine.

Unspoken Love

An unspoken love nobody knew,
A Tom-and-Jerry kind of love,
Running us back into the house,

An unspoken love,
Full of feelings and emotions,
A devotion to timing.

An unspoken intimacy of,
A hug or kiss,

An unspoken love,
Finishing one another's thoughts,
Thoughts of fear that never allowed us,

To be the unspoken love,
We wanted to be.

I am in Love

I am in love with a man,
A man with a master plan,
A Plan to Hold My Hand,
Into the land full of quicksand,

Swallowing my hopes and dreams.
Waiting on tomorrow that never seems...To come,
I am in love,
He is the one,

The one to send my mind into a spiral,
Making my thoughts go viral,
With feelings and emotions,
Repeatedly sending me notifications,

Of all the thoughts that lay in silence between us,
Yes, between us! Yes, between us!

Between us is the other woman,
The woman you hold so dearly,
Working hard to convince me,
That she is bad—she makes you sad,

Playing on my emotions,
Sinking in your lies of devotion,
With gifts,
Working hard to keep your myths,

Yet you stay, yet you stay,
Stay anyway,
Stay anyway, you are in love,
In love with the other woman,

Stop!

Stop stringing me along with the same old song,
Repeated and rehearsed refrain... Boy, you made me
curse,
Boy, please!
Bow down on your knees,
These tears are for me to rise to be the queen,

The queen I needed to be,
I am in love, I am in love,
In love with myself,
Something I never felt before, so I am closing the door
between us,

Yes, between us! Yes, between us!

I deserve more than to share you with other women,
If you cared, I would be your queen... and you be my
king,
To rise together,
We've got to do better,

To conquer true love between man and woman,
I am in love, I am in love,
In love with myself!

Ladies' Choice

A Mother's Pain

A mother's pain is like no other,
Fearing the world will bring grief and sorrow,
From the contractions during birth,
To the unexplained joy when you land on the earth.

Protect the pain she feels inside,
Every time you cried,
Once the adventures of life change as you grow older,
Now, you are standing shoulder-to-shoulder.

A mother's pain is so full of speculation of your choices,
Investigating like a crime scene investigator,
Down the rabbit hole of good and bad intentions,
But still understanding that everything happens for a
reason,

As you overcome emotional discord,
Processing your feelings with the help of a mother's
love,
Helping you discover the devotion as it is poured,
Into a mother's child as pure a dove.

Influential Woman
I am an influential woman,
Crusading ahead for those behind me,
Sailing through choppy water of mayhem,
Searching for the answers to my dreams.

I am an influential woman,

Navigating turmoil that makes my goals seem
intangible,
As I purposely create history,
With resilience and determination,
To restore the confidence of the women behind me.

I am an influential woman,
Providing support like a 911 dispatcher,
Answering my call to encompass my purpose,
In a way to bring shine to historical events.

I am an influential woman,
Influencing future generations,
To make a difference,

By changing the narrative,
That is imperative for us to grow,
As one nation under God,
And we are no longer divisible.

I am an influential woman breaking the glass ceiling,
Investing in strength and unity,
To build a circle of women,
That is influential, unique, and chic.

Gap

Missing out on inspiration,
Because your world is covered in condensation,
Blind to possibilities,

Of what you can truly be,
A doctor, lawyer, even an entrepreneur,
Your vision is limitless,
If only you could see through God's lenses.

A world of endless opportunities,
Breaking glass ceilings that limit your ability,
Stepping out of the box,
Miming your success with gridlocks.

Attempting to block your blessing,
Faith is the best thing,
Staging a revolution,
Where women are no longer fighting for equal pay in
institutions,

But providing financial solutions
To close the gap in distribution.

R.O.A.R

Resilience of an innocent child,
Overcoming the Boogeyman under the bed,
Awareness of an adult,
Restoring calmness and joy.

International Women's Day

A day to celebrate,
The ideology of a phenomenal woman advocating our
vulnerability,
Fighting for equality,

Forging with diversity,
Courageous in every step as you can see,
An International...tribal...empowered woman,
Uncommonly leading her expedition...often
misunderstood and always wished.

For transformation to get everyone listening,
Collectively we are the epitome,
Of innovation and tranquility,
A Global Woman.

Achieving inclusion for you and me,
My body, my choice,
Deciding on what she believes in,
International women, supporting what we have
achieved.

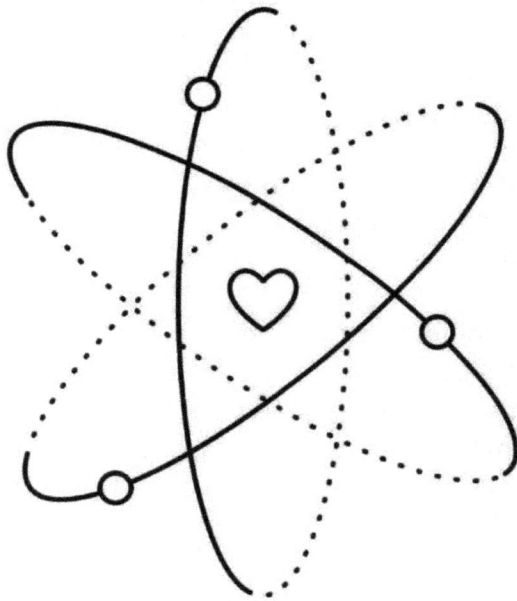

Inspirational Vision

Hope

Hope is depicted in many things,
Based on the joy life brings,
Through memories and time.
We spend imprinting where we have been,

Projecting new steps to where we are going,
Hoping for a successful future.
Based on what life is revealing,
Unveiling our accomplishments,

Caring in love and reciprocation,
Whether you are friends, family, or partner.
Hope over fear, which is harder,
Overcoming past events,

Regaining self-love and kindness trends,
Looking in the rearview mirror,
Reflecting on how far you have grown,
Elevating from the lesson's life has shown.

Rain

As I sit watching this dark storm,
 -I noticed the rain hitting the windowpane.

I relax noticing the minor details of each drop as it,
falls and rolls down the windowpane.

 -Some roll in a straight line,
some with a small hill, and some with multiple hills.
The falling of- the rain rolling down the windowpane is
God's reminder,
Everyone has a different path in life: some on one
accord walking with God,
Some with a minor hill they must climb to walk with
God,
While some with multiple hills we repeatedly climb.

We are all works in progress in our journey with God in
his construction zone.

Whatever your path, God reminds us in the storm that,
No matter how hard it hits you, the path is laid out for
you.
Just roll like the rain and the calm will come.

Fog

Day by day, month by month, year by year, we go
through the fog.

Have you ever really thought about the fog?
It is thick and blinding, and
You do not know what lies on the other side.
Yet we keep going, walking, running, and riding.

We press and press to see the other side.

Fog is our relationship with God.

When we are in the spirit,
we press on by reading,
working, and allowing God to drive.

As we press through life,
Do not forget that God will send you
A message—in the smallest way—to lift a little bit of the
fog daily.
Open your mind, heart, and spirit to allow your fog to
lift.

Wind

Sitting on the porch
 -I felt a breeze putting me at ease.
The gentle touch reminds me,
so much of God's touch—calm but,
strong and comforting.

 -You cannot help but notice.
The wind is,
God's way of touching,
His children in many ways.

 -As parents we let,
Our children know,
they are loved,
and protected every single day.

The wind shows us God's way of saying,
"I am here." His touch can be,
gentle enough to blow paper,
strong enough to bend trees,
or disciplined enough to bring you to your knees.

However, it appears,
that the breeze feels like God is there during it all.

Fire

As the flame inside me starts to die, I sit and wonder
why.

I cry,
God, where are you?
God where are you?!

Is it true you will never,
leave me nor forsake me?

Deliver me from this tragedy, build me,
fire, I want to go higher.

I am down on my knees, please!

God, can't you see, I cry! I cry, deliver me from this
empty place.

I am,
lost in this human race.
As I chase a place of peace.

Hide and Seek

Seek and you will find,
Genuine love,
With the purest intentions,
Oh, did I forget to mention?

This is not on Earth,
It has been with you since birth,
Agape love, spiritual love, unconditional love,
Hard pressed from above.

Intentionally not contingent on what you can do,
Contributing to what is true,
Resurrected just for you,
Omnipresent to your past, present, and future virtue.

Everywhere and nowhere,
As transparent as the air,
Breathing new life into every living thing,
Like the caress of the wind, a tenderness made
intriguing,

The curiosity of someone so,
light and mighty,
In addition to all-seeing,
Hiding in plain sight,
Patiently, waiting for you to seek,
the presence of the omnipotent.

Sandstorm

The wind is whipping,
Smacking my face,
Like sandblasting grit from a steel suitcase,
I have dust in my eyes.

For it blinds the view,
Forgive me if I trip over you,
As I turn my back towards the current,
Slowly my eyelids are free,

I was blind but now, I can see,
Beyond what once tried to stop me,
A tornado of the past,
Except the twister does not last.

Just as you wipe particles from your gaze,
It is a new year, not a phase,
Underneath all the debris and rubble,
Your shine is so bright you no longer struggle.

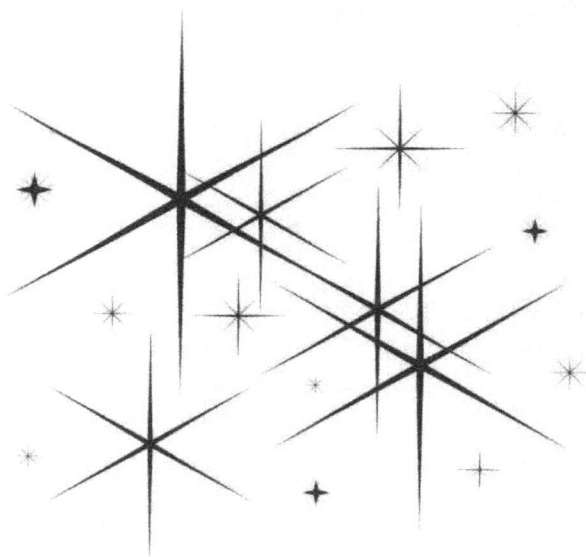

The Success of a New Year

Oh, Glittery Ball

Oh, glittery ball,
You are attracting attention,
Catching the eyes like a chain reaction,
Lighting up the scene with your beaming LED lights,

Influencing lively activities highlights,
Delightful yet indulging,
With the versatility of your appearance,
And an array of your colorful ever so radiant glow.

Putting onlookers in the mood,
With your beautiful reflection,
Bouncing off each glass of cheer,
Gorgeously magnificent evolving with each calendar
year.

As you amplify another year around the sun,
Joyous in celebration counting down with fun,
We eagerly await you to slide down the pole,
Into a New Year as the world turns one more year old.

Finish Strong

Pop goes the starting gun,
Fighting for number one,
Running at your own pace,
Have fun as you race.

Two hundred meters in your lane,
With the speed of Sha 'Carri Richardson, you are left
untamed,
Validating your capability with your agility,
Because you are in the validation of your elite status.

Focused beyond the right or the left,
As you are only in competition with yourself,
Overcoming opposition by being the best you can be,
Making strides with a dash shutting down negativity,

Clocking time as you end two thousand twenty-three,
Cheering with integrity,
As you cross the finish line,
In first place, the race finished strong.

Time and Space of a Calendar

How did the calendar start?
With pages of one, two, and three works of art,
Building months, days, and eventually a week,
Of any particular year that you seek.

Seasonal information created by a pioneer,
A Latin kalendarium collected over time and shared,
Taking account chronological development,
Periods with measurement,

Utilizing moon phases immersing in their brilliant shine,
Evolving from the Egyptian creative mind,
Developing the Julian Calendar growing over 1500
years,
Opening doors for others to mirror.

Gregorian Diary adopted by Europeans,
Babylonians, Jews, and Greeks guided Pope Gregory III
for improvement reasons,
Counting days with simplicity,
Timeframe Lunar in February.

A collaboration of Numa Pompilius,
Festivities help by Quinquatrus,
The solar cycle decided by Julius Caesar,
Creating the ephemeris final Julian table to be a keeper.

Motivation for a New Year

Nervously you await,
Every step you must take,
Armed with the terror of uncertainty,

Yearning to execute your vision successfully,
Each day making it clear,
Achieving your purpose through faith over fear,
Restoring your spirituality claiming you are blessed
beyond your beliefs.

A Successful New Year

Creation of unity,
Built with cultural diversity,
The gray area of liberty,
A new year of hope and glee.

Learning through customs and traditions,
fireworks in unison followed by the loud ringing of
church bells,
Various Earthly time zones and well-wishing,
Remembrance of the past moving forward with good
decisions.

A season of new beginnings,
Wintery weather sparkling lights glistening,
Gathering for future prospering,
Watering a future full of shillings,

Planting seeds for blossoming,
Completing projects, you put your heart and soul in,
Fulfilling obligations to build great positioning,
365 days of helping you win,

Through bridges of humanity,
Fellowship refueling your dream,
One day full of love,
Where fear is not the winner, but a friendly hug.

Conception

Twenty years vicennial,
Miles an hour in a car,
A growing friendship so near, yet so far,
The size of your pants growing after food festivities,
Money is used to purchase necessities.

Celebrating an anniversary of what you achieved,
Added twenty-four is one more year of closing the door,
On the obstacles of twenty-three following goals, you
want to reach,
With purposeful reflections of letting go,
building a new vision, you come to undergo.

Resolution

Oh, resolution where does time go?
From day one, we made a purposeful decision to grow,
Weight loss, nutrition contending to keep up the
tradition,
Giving quality to a new year with ambition.

Whether Eastern or Western we are determined,
To create a world of best practices with self-
determination,
Showing our behavior to improve our physical and
mental health with admiration,
Accomplishing unwavering and admirable self-
preservation,

Foreseeing a historical convention of future
conversations,
Unwritten word of mouth provoking by pledging a
decision,
Promising yourself a good fortune with conviction,
Considering the purpose of the mission,

Allowing yourself to refocus on past commitments,
To improve dedication,
Making investments with excitement and fulfillment,
Dictation of enhancing your life's undesired traits by
reflection and self-evaluation.

January

Julian calendar
A solar cycle of
New beginnings
Undecember as the 13th-month imprinting
Adjusting financial statements of
Roman God's celebration
Year of prosperity and hope for all.

A New Year of Preparation

Discerning through observation a social party
accommodation,
A merriment of festivities,
Full of laughter,
Having hung over the day after,

New Year's Eve is a world celebration,
Last day of the year dedication,
Music, fireworks, and loud explosions made in
preparation.

Sumptuous social delights, appetizer bites,
Champagne toast midnight highlights,
Mailing invites,
Guest arriving dancing until greeted by the sunlight

Holiday history with cultural diversity,
Of spruced-up trees,
With party hats, clocks, metallic décor,
A Russian Primal display of roar.

Celebration

Glaring lights are so bright,
Filling the darkness with luring delight.
From the sparkle of your gold,
With purple, pink, and yellow in your metallic fold.

A fixture in Times Square,
Bringing joyfulness of thunder clapping in the air,
Together under frigid temperatures,
Bundled in coats and hats elegantly embroidered,

Counting down from ten,
Five, four, three, two, and one the year has ended,
With a sixty-second descent,
Blaring crowds gathered, full of cheer ready to ascend,

As confetti fell in conjunction with streamers,
The holiday observance entertained with celebrity
features,
High up in the sky, fireworks flare,
While the crowd yelled out "Happy New Year"!

Color of New Year 2024

There is a place in your heart,
All warm and fuzzy overflowing with compassion,
A gentle touch of love from the jumpstart,
Showing empathy and sharing sweetness in ration,

Nurturing souls with warm kisses,
Enriching the healthiness of the body,
Embracing velvety beauty with blissfulness,
Delighting pastels of cohesiveness,

For the year 2024,
A global color to relax the mind,
Imagining a world ready to explore,
Oh, fuzzy peach you created something uniquely
designed,

From food to clothing,
You are the peacefulness of the year,
A Response to the salutation "How are you doing?"
They are elegantly released as the color of the New Year.

Party Goals

Good gracious the lights are bright,
Blinding smiles and sparkling faces,
Impressive hats trimmed in gold,
With party favors as the world turns one more year old.

Three hundred sixty-five days around the sun,
As we celebrate the last day with lots of fun,
Laughter, noise makers repeatedly blowing whistles,
Shots without chasers drank by midnight dismissal,

Glasses raised as well wishes fade,
Like the fog on a rainy day,
As an umbrella covering your line of thinking,
like tree branches creating shade.

Sinking thoughts after trips and falls,
While climbing ropes out of pitfalls,
Into a flourishing future,
Threading new year's goals like a thread of a suture.

Freeness of a New Year

Watching the roll of a wave,
Getting lost in the crystalline sand,
Quieting my mind slowly silencing everything around
me,
As the rolling water hits like the crackling sound of
thunder,

With a feeling of liberation,
To a full body relaxation,
Through every inhale and exhale,
Filling my body with peace and tranquility,

This is what a new year means to me.

Family Fun

In the darkness of a silent night,
Gathered under the midnight sky,
A family watching as time went by,
Creating memories against gusts of wind.

Dressed in winter coats watching the snowfall,
As the moonlight sparkles hit the softness of the snow,
Bringing a chilly feel into the air while we wait on the
ball,
With a blaring television tuned in to the New Year's Eve
show.

Beneath the noise under the glaring of Grandpa's
campfire; bellies full of laughter,
Despite the cold thermostats, full of hot cocoa, upon
the countdown shortly after.
Whoopsie daisy hot chocolate spilled between the
seats as the children ran past us,
Silly family fun is so full of positive energy that time is
precious.

Giggles of snow angels in the untouched snowfield,
With the waving of the arms and scissors of the legs, an
imprint is made,
Counting down from ten as the family yelled in unison,
Happy New Year to all and may prayer remain at
centerfield!

Liquidation

This is a pleasure for you,
Which brings happiness inside,
With the quench of your thirst and a pucker of the lips,
Fulfilling a dry thirst differently with every sip,

As you put swag into a step,
At the same time, it was so full of chill.
Although you consume what I feel
With the tasting of your sweet liquid even of tart.

No pun intended, you are working from the start,
Your satisfying flavor,
As a cultural staple,
Across the world, there is some form of you shared with
a neighbor,

In celebration of New Year's Eve please drink
responsibly,
No dancing on the table even in the streets,
By now you have met someone new, it was nice to meet
you,
Strawberry Spritzer, Peach Lemonade, or Berry Jupiter
Fizz instead of champagne,
However, no matter how much you enjoy them,
tomorrow's hangover is solely to blame.

Gratitude for the New Year

For nothing is given, nothing is taken,
For a gift is an experience that is unwavering,
From the selection of what will be,
To the sentimental value based on what you believe.

An exception of someone else's desire,
Their individuality of life's gift to everybody,
A story that can only be told,
With your vision and voice,
The blessing of what it means to have a choice.

Your thoughts influence what you will become,
New beginnings for every year start on day one,
Through prayer, things are made clear,
With a feeling of appreciation inside without any regret,
An exception to a New Year you will learn to accept.

Time Flies

Wow! How time flies,
Three hundred sixty-five days went by,
Like a flash of lightning,
The year is gone.

Twelve months, you did not last long,
You stuck around to share your message,
Reflect, remember, and clean up the wreckage.

Restoring the collapse of the economy,
Fifty-two weeks of dichotomy,
Like a math equation of division,
Change the narrative to a new beginning,
Less screaming and shouting, more listening.

Time Square

In the tenebrous night,
A light shines so brightly,
Like a glittery ball,
Set up high, ready to fall.

In seconds, confetti, and sparkles,
Smacking lips, champagne tips,
Bubbly glasses shortly after,
Fireworks echoed with the flow of a throttle.

Controlling the crowd with the police watching,
Prepared and ready for unknown events,
Safety first is everyone's intent,
As we join linking arms while humbly,

Singing with joy to our hearts' content,
Positive words of encouragement,
New lease on life,
Leaving behind the past strife.

New Year's Traditions Haikus

Toast to you,
Clinking glasses,
Champagne splashes,
A New Year's Eve Celebration.

🍎

A couple display,
Kissing lips,
12 o'clock.
Should Auld Acquaintance be Forgot?

🍎

Clocking bells,
Twelve grapes,
Midnight strikes,
Las doce uvas de la suerte.

🍎

Old dishes,
Hurling crockery,
Friends and loved ones,
Broken Plates.

🍎

Pouring water,
Talcum powder,
Blessing sharing,
Talc Smearing.

New Year

"New year new me,"
A time to be free,
Releasing the past,
Moving forward to the future,

With an unknown destination of new beginnings and
untold stories ready to unfold,
Triumph, victory, and even the ones that are scary,
The year of education,
Free lessons from past transgressions.

Evolving into a better me,
A place where I can be free,
To show authenticity,
With self-acceptance unconditionally,

Loving to move forward into my destiny,
Creating a purposeful placement,
Of newness building a futuristic place where I feel
relieved,
By releasing my scream of a Happy New Year!

ABOUT THE AUTHOR

Yasmin S Brown launched her publishing career in 2018 and grew to become an International Best-Selling Author and poet. She also published an extended line of books and contributed to several poetry anthologies. Brown's stories provide personal growth to readers. She is a Guinness World Record participant and has been featured in several magazines including Shout Atlanta, Intellectual Ink, RPG Muse, and Soul Pitt Magazine.

She trained through Toastmasters International to polish her skills as a public speaker. There she combined compassion and empathy for others at her public speaking events. Through this, she received her Distinguished Toastmaster (DTM) award.

While striving to be effective through her work, Yasmin founded Power Her Forward Ltd., a proud sponsor of Yiry-Elements LLC. She is dedicated to advocating for women's mental health, as a certified life coach, specializing in trauma and resilience. As a public speaker and healthcare professional, Yasmin draws on her personal and career experiences to assist others in life, business, and community. She utilizes literacy to encourage women to move forward through the concept of R.O.A.R. (Restoration, Overcome, Awareness, Resilience).

Contact: Yiry Elements Website
Social Media:
Yiry Elements - Facebook
Yiry Elements-Instagram

Previous Publications

Books Written by Yasmin S. Brown:

The Silent Destruction (Deliverance Book 1) (2018)

The Point of Abuse (Deliverance Book 2) (2019) Higher Ground Books & Media

Deliverance: Taquayasia's Final Journey (The Deliverance Series Book 3) (2019) Higher Ground Books & Media

The Iced Tea of Friendship (2020) Higher Ground Books & Media

I Just Want to Be Normal (2020) Higher Ground Books & Media

Hush: Breaking the Chains of Abuse (2024)

Contributor for the Following Publications:

Diamonds In the Rough - A Woman's Guide to Living an Empowered Life (2019) Diamonds in The Rough Enterprises

Voices of the 21st Century: Resilient Women Who Rise and Make a Difference (2021) WSA Publishing

The Talk: Vital Expressions and Conversations by Families of Color (2023) Garden of Neuro Publishing

Diamonds In the Rough - A Woman's Guide to Living an Empowered Life (2019) Diamonds in The Rough Enterprises

A Safe and Brave Space: Anthology of Poetry and Art, Volumes 2 and 3 (2023, 2024) Garden of Neuro Publishing

World Healing World Peace 2024 (2024) Inner Child Press

Armchair Poetry: The Flowers and Butterflies Edition (2023) Inner Child Press, Ltd.

Myths and Legends, An Extraordinary Collection (2023) McKinley Publishing Hub

Love of Longing, An International Anthology of Poems

MANUSHATVAM: Songs of Humanity (We Rise by Lifting Others) (2023) Authorspress

Zaneta Varnado Johns

Zaneta Varnado Johns is a world-class author of three poetry collections and *What Matters Journal*. She has co-authored five international bestselling collaborative books and co-edited three poetry anthologies. Johns is an editor of *Fine Lines Journal* and Women Speakers Association Poet Laureate. Johns resides in Colorado, USA. ZanExpressions.com